Las Posadas
An Hispanic Christmas Celebration

by Diane Hoyt-Goldsmith

photographs by Lawrence Migdale

Holiday House – New York

Library of Congress Cataloging-in-Publication Data

Hoyt-Goldsmith, Diane.

　　　Las Posadas: an Hispanic Christmas celebration / by Diane Hoyt-Goldsmith; photographs by Lawrence Migdale.

　　　　　　　p. cm.

　　　Includes index.

　　　Summary: Follows an Hispanic American family in a small New Mexican
community as they prepare for and celebrate the nine-day religious festival
which occurs just before Christmas.

　　　ISBN 0-8234-1449-3

　　　1. Posadas (Social custom)—New Mexico—Juvenile literature.
2. Christmas—New Mexico—Juvenile literature. 3. Hispanic Americans—Social life and customs—
Juvenile literature. 4. New Mexico—Social life and customs—Juvenile literature. [1. Posadas (Social custom)
2. Christmas—New Mexico. 3. Mexican-Americans—Social life and customs. 4. New Mexico—Social life and
customs.] I. Migdale, Lawrence, ill. II. Title.

GT4986.N6H69 1999

394.266—dc21

99-17337
CIP
AC

　　　ISBN 0-8234-1635-6 (pbk.)

This book is dedicated to
Sister Angelina (Angie) Gonzalez
of la Iglesia de Santa Cruz de la Cañada
in Santa Cruz, New Mexico,
for her leadership in preserving the tradition
of Las Posadas and its celebration
by the people of the Española Valley.

Acknowledgments

We would like to thank the many people who have helped to make this book possible. First of all, thanks to Kristen Lucero and her parents, Ronnie and Francine Huerta, to her grandparents Susan and Frank Roybal, to Bianca, and to the rest of their large and enthusiastic family, for making us feel welcome and for sharing the celebration of Las Posadas with us in their homes and community.

We wish to thank Sister Angie Gonzalez for teaching us about the holiday. Father Ron Carrillo made great contributions to our understanding and appreciation of the celebration. Father José María Blanch arranged the music so our readers could recreate the melodies of this holiday wherever they live. All the nuns of the Holy Cross convent—Sister Lucille Leannah, Sister Thomas Estelle Bryan, Sister Angelina Gonzalez, and Sister John Therese Kusba—all of the Dominican Sisters of Grand Rapids, Michigan, and Sister David Patrick of School Sisters of Notre Dame were always kind and hospitable, making our stay very pleasant. We thank all the people of la Iglesia de Santa Cruz de la Cañada who made us so welcome, especially all those who hosted Las Posadas in their homes: 1st night, Joe and Martha Maestas; 2nd night, Frank and Susie Roybal; 3rd night, Viola Martinez and Abby Jaramillo; 4th night, Helen Vigil, Joe and Mary Martinez; 5th night, the Dominican Sisters from the Convent of la Iglesia de Santa Cruz de la Cañada; 6th night, the Catholic Daughters of la Iglesia de Santa Cruz de la Cañada; 7th night, Plaza de Santa Fe; 8th night, Ruben and Sylvia Garcia; 9th night, Father Ron and Father Blanch at the Rectory of la Iglesia de Santa Cruz de la Cañada. Thanks to Ruben Garcia, Jr., who played the part of Joseph, and his parents, Sylvia and Joseph Garcia.

The celebration would not be the same without the contributions of the musicians who played each night for Las Posadas: Teofilo Martinez, Teodora Valdez, Larry Ulibarri, Eulogio Serrano, Bernie Jaramillo, and Jerry Allarid.

We have a special debt of thanks to Felix Lopez and his talented family: his wife, Luisa, who shared the art of tin work, his son Joseph, who taught us more about the carving of bultos, and daughter Krissa, who showed us the craft of straw appliqué. In addition, we are grateful to Manuel Lopez and his daughter Renee, who showed us the art of retablo painting. We appreciate the time we were able to spend with Sam Montoya, learning more about the chapel dedicated to San Ysidro. Thanks to Robin Farwell Gavin of the Museum of International Folk Art in Santa Fe, New Mexico, and Ernest and Rita Duarte of Tucson, Arizona, who gave us invaluable assistance when this project was still just an idea.

For proofreading and translation of the song for Las Posadas, we wish to thank Pamela A. Lim-McAlister, M.A., a teacher of Spanish language and literature at the University of California, Berkeley Extension, and Vista College.

Each year, as night falls on December 15, people in the town of Española, New Mexico, observe a very special tradition. Led by young people dressed as Mary and Joseph from the Bible, they participate in Las Posadas (LAS poh-SAH-dahs), a religious celebration that occurs just before Christmas.

This year, an eleven-year-old girl named Kristen will be Mary on one of the nine nights of the festival. Kristen lives with her mother and stepfather near La Mesilla (LAH may-SEE-ah), New Mexico. Like many other people who live here, she worships in the Catholic church in Santa Cruz, a small nearby town.

Kristen lives close to her grandparents and visits them almost every day. She sits on her grandfather's stallion named Gabino. Kristen's grandfather and her aunt Bianca are teaching her how to ride and to care for the horses on the ranch.

Las Posadas is part of the Spanish heritage of this part of New Mexico. Once a part of New Spain, settlers from Mexico came to live here in 1598. They built homes, planted crops, and raised cattle. They brought their Catholic faith with them to their new home. Catholic priests also came to teach the Native Americans about Christianity. The people helped them build missions and churches throughout the countryside. Many of these very old churches still exist.

Many of today's residents in the towns of La Mesilla, Española, and Santa Cruz are ancestors of those first Spanish settlers. Although most people speak English, many families, like Kristen's, speak Spanish, too.

Kristen likes to practice guitar and sing Spanish songs in her grandfather's hay barn.

NEW MEXICO

RIO CHAMA

ABIQUIU

RIO GRANDE

TAOS

LAS TRUCHAS

CHIMAYO

SANTA CRUZ

ESPAÑOLA

LA MESILLA

LOS ALAMOS

SANTA FE

N
W E
S

The church at Santa Cruz is called la Iglesia de Santa Cruz de la Cañada.

In 1733, Spanish settlers began the construction of a church in Santa Cruz. In those days, the church was the center of community life. Everyone belonged to it and took part in its festivals, feast days, and masses. People came to church to worship, but it was also a place to meet socially. Built of adobe, the church faced the main plaza in the town.

Kristen and her family attend this ancient church today. Although the community is more diverse now than it was a hundred years ago, for many people like Kristen, the church at Santa Cruz is still a focus for their lives.

The interior of the church at Santa Cruz is decorated with many beautiful paintings and carvings of saints. Some are several hundred years old.

On Sundays, Kristen is an altar server in the church. She helps the priest, Father Ron Carrillo, during the service.

Photo courtesy of Tom Velarde

Kristen and her parents help to take care of the chapel.

Long ago, before there were automobiles, people went to church on foot or on horseback. Many people lived far away from town, so neighbors joined together to build small chapels near their homes. Then they could worship every day. In La Mesilla, not far from the house where Kristen's grandparents live, is a small chapel built by the people in that community. It is just one of many small chapels found all around Santa Cruz. Although it is easy for people to go to church today, the chapels are still used for special feast days and celebrations.

The people in the community work together to maintain the chapel buildings. Kristen's parents are the *major duomos* (MY-yor DWO-mohs), the people in charge of organizing the work. Kristen spends many hours helping them. The chapel in La Mesilla is dedicated to San Ysidro (SAN ee-SEE-dro), the patron saint of farmers.

Figures of saints, called *santos* (SAHN-tohs) in Spanish, are very important to the people who worship in the Catholic Church. They have been used in chapels and churches since Spanish colonial times in New Mexico. Each church and chapel has many representations of saints. Some are carved from wood. Others are portraits painted on wooden panels. The santos represent holy persons who have died but whose lives provide examples for the faithful. Each image embodies the qualities of the saintly person in some way. The saint can be identified by the symbols in the carving or painting. For example, San Ysidro is a farmer. He is always shown in a simple frock coat. In one hand, he holds a shaft of wheat to symbolize the crops. The bag at his waist contains seeds for sowing. In the other hand, he holds a tool that was used to keep the oxen moving. The angel pushing the plow comes from the legend of San Ysidro's life.

The Legend of San Ysidro
The Patron Saint of Farmers

Ysidro was born in 1070 near Madrid, Spain. He came from a very poor family. When he grew up, he went to work on the estate of a wealthy man. Ysidro lived at a time when all the crops belonged to the king. The common people had very little. Ysidro lived a life of devotion to God. He set an example, always sharing what he had with others. Because of his devotion to God, Ysidro spent his days in prayer, rather than working in the fields for the king. Even so, his fields were always plowed and ready for planting. One night, the king sent soldiers to arrest him. As they came near his house, they saw oxen working in the fields. An angel stood behind the plow, finishing Ysidro's work. Meanwhile, Ysidro was lost in prayer. Ysidro was made a saint in 1622 and was called San Ysidro ever after.

Kristen's neighbor, Felix Lopez, and his son Joseph, carve santos. They are called *santeros* (sahn-TAY-rohs). This folk art tradition began in the early days of Spanish settlement. Recently, the craft has had a revival because there are so many old churches and chapels in the area that need to be restored.

Felix works on a new santo of the Virgin of Guadalupe, while his son Joseph carves a large figure of Moses.

Like the santeros of long ago, Felix Lopez uses materials found in nature to make his paint. He uses indigo plants for blue, soot from the fireplace for black, and red and yellow clay to make red and yellow paint. Cochineal, a tiny insect, is ground up to make a bright red color. Resin from the piñon tree is combined with alcohol as a binder for these pigments. Felix makes gesso, a white mixture used to prepare the wood for painting, from gypsum rocks that he finds while walking in the fields.

Carvers make santos to give people images of saints. Seeing them in church, people look on the santos as they would friends. Often, people entering the church greet the santos, as if saying hello to someone special. Having a santo in the church makes people feel as if the spirit of that holy person is there.

Santeros have always been valued in the Hispanic communities in New Mexico. Long ago, people had to survive on what they could grow or raise. They faced forces over which they had no control, like bad weather or natural disasters. The carvings of the saints made the people feel connected to God. They could pray to the santos for help.

Santos are usually carved from pieces of cottonwood or aspen. First the wood is shaped into a roughly carved figure. Then the special symbols of the santo are carved and added. It takes many, many weeks to make a santo.

Krissa Lopez shows Kristen how to make straw appliqués. The designs look like intricate inlaid wood designs from Italy and Spain in the 16th century.

Kristen's community is rich in folk art traditions. One of these is called straw appliqué or *paja embutida* (PAH-hah em-boo-TEE-dah) in Spanish. It is a way to make beautiful objects out of very common materials. Straw from wheat is cut into geometric shapes. Soot or walnut husks soaked in water are mixed with rabbit skin glue to make a dark, sticky surface on which the straw pieces are placed. The light-colored straw contrasts with the dull black of the surface to create a design on wooden boxes or crosses.

Kristen's friend Renee has been painting pictures of the saints, called *retablos* (reh-TAH-blohs), since she was six years old. These portraits are found in Catholic churches and in homes. They are used for devotions and prayers.

15

The History of Las Posadas

Las Posadas has been celebrated in Mexico and a few other countries in Latin America for centuries. Communities in the United States, where Spanish cultural influence is strong, observe this holiday, too. Most of these celebrations take place in the southwest, in New Mexico, Texas, Arizona, and California.

Las Posadas began more than four hundred years ago in Spain. Priests wanted to teach the people about the Bible. However, at that time, most people could neither read nor write. The priests found that the best way to help them learn the Bible stories was to act the stories out.

Some of these dramas took the form of *novenas* (noh-VEH-nahs), a Latin word meaning "nine each." Novenas are prayers that are repeated for nine days in a row. Las Posadas means "the inns" in Spanish. The Las Posadas novena tells the story of Mary and Joseph and their visit to Bethlehem at the time when Jesus was born. The story of Las Posadas can be found in the Holy Bible.

Luke, Chapter 2, Verses 1-7.

It came to pass that the ruler of Judea, Augustus Caesar, declared that all the world should be taxed. Each person had to return to his or her place of birth to pay the tax. Mary, although expecting the birth of her first child, was obliged to travel with Joseph to Bethlehem. They made the journey on a donkey.

When they arrived in Bethlehem, the city was full of other travelers. They went from place to place, from inn to inn, looking for a place to stay. Unfortunately, there was no room anywhere. Finally, desperate for a place to rest, they came to an inn where the owner said they could make their beds with the animals in his stable.

So amid the animals resting in the night, Mary and Joseph made their beds. Late that night, in these humble surroundings, the baby Jesus was born.

People like to celebrate Las Posadas because it prepares them for Christmas. From December 15 until December 23, Las Posadas is celebrated each night. This tradition puts the emphasis back on the Christmas story and away from the gifts, commercialism, and the other things that can distract believers from the true meaning of Christmas.

Kristen shows her cousin their grandmother's Nativity scene.

Kristen helps her mother, her grandmother, and her great-grandmother make tamales to serve their guests during Las Posadas. They are made from a mixture of meat and chili, wrapped up with *masa* (MAH-sah), a type of corn meal, and then steamed. For Kristen and her family, it wouldn't be Las Posadas without tamales.

Getting Ready for Las Posadas

Kristen has been celebrating Las Posadas for as long as she can remember. This year is special because she will play the part of Mary on one of the nine nights. Her grandparents also are hosting the people from the church at their home in La Mesilla.

For weeks, the whole family works together to make food to feed their guests. They will serve *tamales* (tah-MAH-lays), *posole* (poh-SOH-lay), which is a type of roasted-corn soup, and *biscochitos* (bis-coh-CHEE-tohs), Kristen's favorite holiday cookie.

Biscochitos
Cookies for Las Posadas

A recipe from the kitchen of Kristen's grandmother Susan Roybal

1/2 cup butter

1/2 cup shortening

1 egg

3/4 cup sugar

1/4 teas. vanilla

3/8 cup sweet chokecherry juice

1/4 teas. salt

1/4 teas. anise

1/4 teas. baking powder

2 3/4 cup flour

1 cup sugar

1 teas. cinnamon

Cream together the butter and shortening until soft. Beat in the egg and sugar until smooth. Mix in the vanilla, cherry juice, salt, anise, and baking powder. Add the flour in small batches, working it in by hand until you have a smooth dough.

Roll the dough out until it is about an 1/8 inch thick. Cut the dough into hearts, flowers, and stars. Dip each cookie in a mixture of the cinnamon and sugar. Bake at 400 degrees for 15 minutes. This recipe makes about five dozen three-inch cookies.

The cookies can be made ahead and kept in the freezer until the day you want to serve them.

19

LA PUEBLA

LA MESILLA

RIVERSIDE

Celebrating Las Posadas

Each of the nine nights of Las Posadas begins in the same way. First, people attend a mass in the church at Santa Cruz. Then, everyone boards a school bus for a ride to the home of the family who will host Las Posadas for the evening. The people will visit a different home each night.

When they arrive, the group is greeted by the host family. The people divide into two groups. One group goes inside the house. They play the part of the innkeepers. The other group remains outdoors in the cold. Those outside play the part of the *peregrinos* (peh-reh-GREE-nohs), or pilgrims. A girl and boy, dressed as Mary and Joseph, take their places in front of the peregrinos at the entrance to the house, ready to come in as soon as they are invited.

Kristen and her parents arrive early at the church before the mass begins. Together they say the Rosary, a special series of prayers.

This is a map of the nine places *peregrinos* will visit for Las Posadas.

Kristen and her friend Ruben play the parts of Mary and Joseph in La Mesilla on the second night of Las Posadas.

Farolitas light the way for
the peregrinos during Las
Posadas.

Farolitas light the way for the peregrinos during Las Posadas.

Kristen's grandfather sets a bonfire next to their home to light the way for the peregrinos. This is called a *luminaria* (LOO-min-AH-ree-ah). Some people light the way for Las Posadas with *farolitas* (FAH-roh-LEE-tahs). These small lights are made from candles set in sand inside paper bags.

To begin, Mary and Joseph knock on the door of the house several times. When the innkeepers answer, they lead the peregrinos in a song that asks for shelter for the night. The group inside answers. They sing a song to complain about being disturbed. Sixteen verses later, each time alternating between the people inside singing and those outside singing, the innkeepers finally invite their guests to come in. Everyone sings the final verses together. Inside the celebration continues with prayers and Christmas carols sung in Spanish.

Once inside, the festivities continue, with more music and prayers.

The Song of Las Posadas

Afuera	Outside
De larga jornada	From a long journey
Rendidos llegamos	Very weary are we
Y así imploramos	We ask you for shelter
Para descansar.	For Mary and me.
¿Quién nos da posada	Who will give lodging
Estos peregrinos	To these travelers so weary?
Que vienen cansados	We are very tired
De andar los caminos?	From trudging roads so dreary.
¿Robaros pretendo	I only intend to ask you
Y es el corazón	From the kindness of your heart
Que a mi esposa amada,	To give my beloved wife a room,
Le deis un rincón?	Just a corner, some small part?
Necesidad grave	Serious necessity
A mi esposa aflige	Distresses my spouse.
Un rincón les pido	I ask you for a corner
Donde se recline.	Please let her rest inside your house.
Hacedlo por Dios.	Do this for the love of God.
Que mi esposa amada	For my beloved wife
Con frío y cansancio	With such cold and weariness
Viene fatigada.	Has never been so tired in her life.
Que esta bella niña	This beautiful maiden
Ya no sufre el hielo,	Can no longer stand the cold
No puede aguantar	She cannot bear the rigors
El rigor del tiempo.	Of this stormy night so bold.
La noche avanza.	For the love of God, be kind,
Por Dios condoleos	Soon night will fall.
Que descanse un poco	Some rest for the Queen of Heaven
La Reina del cielo.	Is what we ask for, that is all.
Es José y María,	It is Joseph and Mary,
Su esposa amada,	His beloved spouse,
Que a tus puertas	Who stand at your doors
Vienen a pedir posada.	And seek lodging in your house.
No tengáis en poco	This sweet act of charity
Esta caridad	Do not take lightly
El cielo benigno	For the kind heavens above
Os compensará.	Will reward you rightly.

Adentro	Inside
¿Quién a nuestras puertas	Who comes to our doors
En noche inclemente	This stormy night?
se acerca imprudente	Who approaches unwisely
Para molestar?	To give us a fright?
¿Quién es quién la pide?	Who asks for lodging?
Yo no la he de dar.	I cannot grant your request.
Si serán ladrones	You could be thieves
Que querrán robar.	Intent on robbing at best.
No hay rincón vacío	There is no vacant corner
Que poder franquear.	That we can rent you.
Vacío está el campo	The fields are free and empty
Y en él hospedar.	So stay out there, please do.
¿Quién es quién perturba	Who is it that disturbs
De noche el sosiego?	This night so calm and deep?
Márchense de aquí	Leave, go away, and do not rob us
No nos quiten el sueño.	Of our dreams and of our sleep.
Qué genta tan necia	Such foolish people,
Ya me está enfadando	My anger at you is deep.
Márchense de aquí	Leave, go away, get out of here.
No estén despertando.	Do not wake us from our sleep.
Ya se ve que es tarde	You can see how late it is
Y venir con eso	And to come with such a request
Se hacen sospechoso.	Makes me quite suspicious of you.
Márchense al momento.	Leave here at once, let us rest.
Ruegos importunos.	Your pleas are annoying.
No, no escucharemos.	No, we will not listen.
Vacío está el campo,	Seek shelter in the empty fields,
Y en él recogeros.	Where the stars so brightly glisten.
Entra, bella niña,	Enter, beautiful maiden,
Tú y tu compañero.	You and your spouse.
Esta es vuestra casa	We offer it to you humbly,
Que humilde ofrecemos.	This is your house.
Abranse las puertas,	Let the doors be thrown open,
Rómpanse los velos,	Let the curtains be torn down,
Que viene a posar	For the Queen of Heaven
La Reina del cielo.	Has come to rest in our town.

La Canción de Las Posadas

Outside, the peregrinos begin by singing . . .

Inside, the innkeepers answer by singing . . .

Las Posadas in the Plaza

The Devil appears to frighten the peregrinos away.

Led by Mary and Joseph, people sing Christmas carols.

One night during Las Posadas, the people from the Church at Santa Cruz go to the Plaza in Santa Fe. Here they celebrate their Christmas tradition in a different way with visitors from all over the world.

For this celebration of Las Posadas, the peregrinos circle the plaza. Instead of visiting a home, they visit each of the four sides of the plaza. Instead of an innkeeper, they are answered by someone dressed as the Devil. He appears suddenly, as if by magic, in a second-story window or on a rooftop. Four times the Devil tells the peregrinos that there is no room for them at the inn and shouts at them to go away.

Mary and Joseph never give up. Finally, they arrive at an enclosed courtyard in the Palace of the Governors. There they find a warm stable with a bed of straw. Nestled there is a Nativity scene with Mary, Joseph, and the baby Jesus. The peregrinos and the public join together to sing Christmas carols in Spanish. They drink hot chocolate and warm themselves at bonfires set to keep away the chill.

During Las Posadas, Kristen joins others in her church youth group to bring food for Christmas dinner to people in need.

For Kristen and her community, the celebration of Las Posadas is a combination of many good things. Some people attend each night of Las Posadas. These people believe that it is important to complete the novena. Others attend as many nights as their busy holiday schedules allow. Everyone agrees, however, that participating in Las Posadas helps them to prepare for Christmas. By taking part in the Christmas story, they experience it in a personal way. By becoming peregrinos and following Mary and Joseph, each person becomes part of the Christmas story.

Each night after all the prayers and songs have been sung, the peregrinos join the evening's host to share a delicious meal. Many of the foods, such as the biscochitos and tamales, are made especially for this holiday. Some families make a delicious dessert called *capirotada* (cah-pee-roh-TAH-dah), also called *sopa* (SOH-pah), a bread pudding that combines raisins, fruit, and cheese. *Chicos* (CHEE-cohs), a dish of parched corn with pork, and *empanadas* (em-pah-NAH-dahs), a pastry filled with apples and other good things, are favorites. No matter what the menu, friends and strangers alike are welcome to share the meal.

After the singing is over, people gather to share a meal.

29

On Christmas Eve, Kristen gives her grandmother a handmade gift.

On Christmas Eve, Kristen and her family exchange gifts. There is usually a special present for each of the children. Because she has celebrated Las Posadas, Kristen knows there are other kinds of gifts, too. There are traditions from her ancestors that help her to know her identity. There are spiritual gifts that bind her to the community and help guide her life. Las Posadas is a holiday that allows Kristen and the others in her community to express the joy of faith, the greatest gift of all.

Glossary

adobe: sun dried bricks made from clay and straw.

biscochitos: (bis-coh-CHEE-tohs) sugar cookies, flavored with anise, that are made to celebrate Las Posadas.

capirotada: (cah-pee-roh-TAH-dah) also called *sopa*, is a bread pudding made with raisins, fruit, and cheese.

chapel: a small building used for religious services and ceremonies.

chicos: (CHEE-cohs) a dish of parched corn cooked with pork.

empanadas: (em-pah-NAH-dahs) a Mexican pie made by baking meat or fruit that has been wrapped in dough.

farolitas: (FAH-roh-LEE-tahs) simple lights used to illuminate a pathway, made from a paper bag with a few inches of sand in the bottom. A candle is lit and placed in the middle of the sand. The light shines out through the paper. The bag keeps the candle from blowing out in the wind.

gesso: a white paint made from baked gypsum rock that is ground up and mixed with rabbit skin glue. It is used to prepare wood for painting.

Hispanic: culturally related to Spain or influenced by Spanish culture.

Las Posadas: (LAS poh-SAH-dahs) a nine-day novena that celebrates the journey through Bethlehem that Mary and Joseph made on the night that Jesus was born.

luminaria: (LOO-min-AH-ree-ah) a small bonfire set along a road or in a front yard during Las Posadas, to light the way for the peregrinos.

major duomo: (MY-yor DWO-moh) the person in charge of organizing the maintenance of a small chapel.

masa: (MAH-sah) corn meal.

Mass: a daily religious service in a Catholic church.

novena: (noh-VEH-nah) a prayer or series of prayers that is repeated for nine days in a row.

paja embutida: (PAH-hah em-boo-TEE-dah) the Hispanic folk art tradition of straw appliqué.

peregrinos: (peh-reh-GREE-nohs) the Spanish term for pilgrims.

posole: (poh-SOH-lay) a soup made from roasted corn.

priest: a religious leader of a Catholic church, who leads the congregation in the Mass.

retablo: (reh-TAH-bloh) a small painting of a saint, used in devotions.

Rosary: a string of beads used to keep a count of a special series of prayers.

San Ysidro: (SAN ee-SEE-dro) the patron saint of farmers.

santero: (sahn-TAY-roh) a person who carves figures of the saints.

santo: (SAHN-toh) a representation of a saint, usually carved in wood, that is used in devotions.

sopa: (SOH-pah) also called *capirotada*, is a bread pudding made with raisins, fruit, and cheese.

tamales: (tah-MAH-lays) A traditional Mexican dish, often served at Christmas, that is prepared with a mixture of meat and chilis with masa, all wrapped in a corn husk and then steamed until cooked.

Index

(Numbers in italics refer to pages with photos or illustrations.)